DUSTPRINTS OF THE RABBI

DISCIPLESHIP IN THE TEXTURE OF TORAH AND GRACE

THE COVENANT PATH™ SERIES
BOOK ONE

RICH VAN DOORN

To my family—
your love, laughter, and faith have steadied my steps and shaped
my soul.
You walk this path with me, and for that I am forever grateful.

And to my dad—
who first pointed me toward the narrow way,
who showed me what it means to follow the Rabbi,
and whose footprints led me closer to the dust of Jesus.
Thank you for walking ahead,
for circling back when I wandered,
and for never stopping until I knew the Way, the Truth, and the
Life.
This book bears the imprint of your example.

CONTENTS

FOREWORD

There is a phrase I heard years ago that arrested my heart and never let go:

"May you be covered in the dust of your Rabbi."

That ancient blessing wasn't poetic fluff—it was an invitation. A challenge. A declaration that true discipleship meant walking so closely behind your teacher that the very dust from His sandals would cling to your skin. It meant a life of proximity, obedience, surrender, and transformation. It meant following—not just believing.

This first book in *The Covenant Path™* series was born from a hunger to return to that kind of discipleship.

Not the casual kind. Not the cultural kind. But the kind that costs something. The kind that changes everything.

For years, I wrestled with what it meant to be a follower of Jesus—not just in theology, but in lifestyle. My journey took me deep into the Jewish roots of our faith, the historical context of the first-century world, and the rich layers of Torah and grace that shaped the lives of His earliest disciples.

Along the way, I discovered that discipleship was never meant to be a class or a creed—it was meant to be a path. A covenant path.

This book doesn't offer easy answers or spiritual shortcuts. It invites you into something deeper. Something ancient. It invites you to lace up your sandals, step into the dust, and follow the Rabbi—not from a distance, but up close. Where His voice is clear. Where His way is costly. Where His dust becomes your covering.

I pray that as you journey through these pages, you'll not only learn about the life of the Rabbi—but you'll start walking like Him. Living like Him. Loving like Him.

Because in the end, the greatest legacy any of us can leave behind is the dust of obedience on someone else's feet.

Let's begin the journey.

—Rich Van Doorn

THE COVENANT PATH™
SERIES MAP

WALKING THE WAY OF THE RABBI — ONE
BOOK, ONE STEP AT A TIME

Your Journey Has Begun...

This Core Book — *Dustprints of the Rabbi* — is just the first step in a 17-book discipleship journey.

Each book in *The Covenant Path*™ series is paired with:

- A **Core Book** – Theological and historical foundations
- A **Devotional** – Six-day spiritual practice + Sabbath reflection
- A **Leader Guide** – Cultural insights, Hebraic terms, and small group support

THE COVENANT PATH™ SERIES (CONFIRMED TITLES & SUBTITLES)

1. **Dustprints of the Rabbi**: *Discipleship in the Texture of Torah and Grace*

HOW TO KEEP WALKING

Each step includes:

- A teaching book
- A companion devotional
- A leader guide like this one

Start with the next title — or gather a new group to walk through this one again.

Discipleship is not a class. It's a path. The Rabbi is still walking. So must we.

INTRODUCTION

IN THE DUST OF HIS FEET

The first disciples did not follow Jesus in comfort. They followed Him in **dust**. It clung to their robes as they trailed behind Him through Galilean towns, gathered on their feet as they listened to parables beneath olive trees, and settled into their hearts as they slowly discovered that following this Rabbi would require everything. And still, they followed.

They followed because they had seen something in Jesus that no one else carried — a flame that lit ancient prophecies, a voice that echoed Sinai, a presence that walked like God once walked among the tents of Abraham and the wilderness of Moses.

This was no ordinary teacher. This was a *Rabbi of the Covenant*. And they would not just learn from Him — they would be remade by Him.

THE COVENANT PATH™ SERIES

Dustprints of the Rabbi is the first of **seventeen books** in **The Covenant Path™**, a discipleship series that invites modern followers of Jesus to walk in the ancient footsteps of their Rabbi.

Each book builds on the next — rooted in Scripture, Jewish history, Hebraic thought, and covenant faithfulness.

This is not a curriculum.

It is not a devotional.

It is a road.

A path.

A covenant journey into a way of living that reshapes every corner of life — your identity, relationships, decisions, and destiny.

WHY THIS SERIES FEELS DIFFERENT

You may notice early on that this book — and this series — feels different from many Western discipleship materials. That's intentional.

The Bible wasn't written in English.

Jesus wasn't a modern preacher.

And discipleship in the first century didn't happen in coffee shops with fill-in-the-blank workbooks.

This series was crafted to invite you into the **world Jesus actually lived in**:

- A world of Rabbis and disciples (*talmidim*)
- Of walking behind, not ahead
- Of covenant patterns, not casual belief
- Of spiritual formation shaped by **Torah**, **prophets**, and the **Shema** — not just modern Christian culture

TERMS YOU'LL SEE

Throughout this book and the entire Covenant Path series, you'll encounter ancient Jewish terms. Here's a quick guide:

- **Torah** (תּוֹרָה): The first five books of the Bible — the core instruction given to Israel. Jesus lived, taught, and fulfilled it.
- **Tanakh** (תַּנַ"ךְ): The complete Hebrew Bible (what Christians call the Old Testament). It includes the Torah (Law), Nevi'im (Prophets), and Ketuvim (Writings).
- **Talmud** (תַּלְמוּד): A collection of rabbinic discussions about how to live out the Torah. It includes rich insights and historical context for understanding the world Jesus lived in.
- **Mishnah** (מִשְׁנָה): The earliest written compilation of Jewish oral law, reflecting how Rabbis trained disciples to live out covenant loyalty in daily life.
- **Midrash** (מִדְרָשׁ): Ancient Jewish interpretive storytelling and commentary — often creative and layered — used to explore deeper meanings in Scripture.

These are not used to complicate, but to **illuminate**. You are not expected to master them — only to **see through them** into a world where following Jesus was an all-consuming walk of covenant obedience.

WHAT THIS BOOK WILL ASK OF YOU

Each chapter includes:

- A **historical immersion** — placing you in the world of the Rabbi
- A **core teaching** — rooted in Scripture and Jewish-Christian theology
- A **modern application and reflection** — to bring ancient truths into today's walk
- A **covenant challenge** — because discipleship was never meant to stay theoretical

This is not a book to be admired.
It is a path to be walked.
You will be challenged.
You may be stretched.
You will not be the same.

YOU ARE NOT ALONE

This is only the beginning. *Dustprints of the Rabbi* lays the foundation for what will follow across sixteen more books — each one exploring a new angle of the covenant journey:

- The Shema life
- Covenant loyalty
- Authority, fire, mercy, obedience, and suffering
- Festivals, wildernesses, callings, and resurrection

Together, these books will help you not just know your faith, but walk it like the *talmidim* did — covered in the dust of the Rabbi.

THE INVITATION REMAINS

Jesus did not say, "Believe Me." He said:

"Come. Follow Me."

If you're ready to walk behind the Rabbi — to let His dust mark your life, to step onto the ancient road and never turn back —then welcome.

The Covenant Path begins here.

DUST ON YOUR FEET

THE CALL TO WALK CLOSELY BEHIND THE RABBI

"Let your house be a meeting house for the Sages, and sit in the dust of their feet, and drink in their words with thirst."

— MISHNAH, AVOT 1:4

SETTING THE SCENE: THE WORLD OF THE RABBI

THE GALILEAN SUN HUNG HEAVY OVER THE NARROW ROAD leading into the village. Dust, pale as ash and fine as flour, clouded beneath the feet of travelers — merchants, farmers, and, tucked among them, a Rabbi and his *talmidim*. His disciples.

They walked in deliberate steps, their sandals kicking up the same dust that had covered Abraham, Moses, and the prophets before them. One foot after another, no fanfare, no crowds — only the rhythm of feet and the murmured recitations of Torah verses carried on the dry, hot wind.

The youngest disciple stumbled slightly on a stone hidden beneath the dirt. He quickly caught himself, looking up to the Rabbi ahead — imitating even the way his master brushed his robe and adjusted his sandals.

To follow a Rabbi meant far more than memorizing words. It meant breathing his breath, imitating his gestures, and absorbing the sacred dust of his journey.

CORE TEACHING: COVENANT DUST AND THE ANCIENT ROAD

Covenant Dust: Not Decoration, but Identification

In the biblical mind, dust is never meaningless. From the beginning, humanity was shaped from the dust of the earth (Genesis 2:7). From dust we are made — and to dust we return (Genesis 3:19). Dust is **origin and destiny** intertwined. Thus, in the Hebraic view, dust is not dirt to be dismissed — it is essence.

To bear someone's dust meant you bore their life, their path, their identity. In the Mishnah, the early rabbis instructed:

"Let your house be a meeting place for the sages, and sit in the dust of their feet, and drink in their words with thirst."

— MISHNAH, AVOT 1:4

Sitting in the dust was not simply about proximity. It was about **submission to covenant teaching** — a heart so thirsty that even the dust shaken loose by the Rabbi's steps became nourishment. In ancient Israel, dust meant more than closeness. It meant **covenantal belonging**.

Discipleship in the First-Century Hebraic World

A *talmid* (תלמיד) — a disciple — in Jesus' day was not merely a learner. He was a covenant follower. The disciple's life was defined by:

- *Devekut* (דְּבֵקוּת): Clinging devotion — staying so near the master that nothing could tear you away.
- *Halakhah* (הֲלָכָה): Walking in the Rabbi's path — not just hearing his words, but embodying his interpretation of Torah in daily life.
- *Mishmeret* (מִשְׁמֶרֶת): Guarding covenant loyalty — living under discipline, accountability, and surrender to the Rabbi's authority.

The disciple's ambition was not to become famous but to be **mistaken for his master**. It was understood that:

- The dust that covered you was **proof** that you walked the Covenant Path.
- The suffering you shared with your Rabbi was **glory**, not shame.

Jesus and the Radical Restoration of Covenant Discipleship

When Jesus said:

"Come, follow Me",

— MATTHEW 4:19

He was offering nothing less than **ancient covenant allegiance**. This was not a call to religious attendance. It was a **Genesis 12 call** — just as Abraham had been called to leave everything behind and walk into covenant promise, so too Jesus' disciples were called to abandon trades, inheritances, and reputations for the sake of following the Messiah.

In Jewish tradition, the first words of a Rabbi to a prospective disciple were vital:

- If the Rabbi believed the student had the capacity to become like him, he would say:

"Lech acharai" (לֵךְ אַחֲרַי) — *"Come, follow me."*

Jesus was using these same words — **but with a Kingdom urgency**:

- Not merely to teach Torah interpretation, but to **reveal and embody the Torah fulfilled**.
- Not to train students, but to **form witnesses who would bear His dust into the nations.**

Hebraic Foundations for Bearing the Rabbi's Dust

In ancient Jewish thought, to walk behind a master meant:

- **Receiving his yoke (ol)** — accepting full submission to his interpretation and lifestyle (cf. Matthew 11:28–30).
- **Absorbing his midrash** — his way of interpreting Scripture and applying it to life.
- **Carrying his shame and honor alike** — enduring what he endured without flinching (cf. Isaiah 50:6–7).

Paul, trained under Rabbi Gamaliel (Acts 22:3), understood this deeply. When he later wrote:

"Follow my example, as I follow the example of Christ."
1 Corinthians 11:1

He was speaking as a Rabbi who knew that to follow meant:

- Dust on the feet.
- Scars on the back.
- Songs in prison cells.

Dust Was Proof of Covenant Endurance

The Hebrew Scriptures consistently link dust with both suffering and glory:

- **Abraham** bowed to the dust (Genesis 18:27) in humble covenant conversation with God.
- **Moses** led a dusty people through a dusty wilderness, toward a promised inheritance (Deuteronomy 8:2–4).

- **The Servant of the LORD** (Isaiah 53) would be marred, despised — and yet would see the fruit of His suffering.

When Jesus bent low to wash His disciples' feet (John 13:5), He washed dust that would soon be stained by betrayal, denial, and fear — and yet He still chose love.
Dust is not merely historical.
It is covenantal.
It is the signature of those who have not turned back.

The Dust Crisis in Modern Christianity

Today, many want the Rabbi's blessings without bearing the Rabbi's dust.

- We seek resurrection without crucifixion.
- We seek anointing without wilderness hunger.
- We seek comfort without covenant.

But the Scriptures are clear:

There is no crown without the dust of Gethsemane.

There is no throne without the dust of Golgotha.

When Jesus taught:

"If anyone would come after me, let him deny himself and take up his cross daily and follow me."

— LUKE 9:23

He was speaking covenant language:

- Walk behind Me.
- Bear My dust.
- Share My suffering.
- Inherit My glory.

Paul understood it perfectly:

"I want to know Christ — yes, to know the power of His resurrection and participation in His sufferings, becoming like Him in His death."

— PHILIPPIANS 3:10

The Invitation: Covenant Dust Awaits

The ancient call remains:

"Lech acharai." ("Come after Me.")

Not into ease —
into dust.
Not into applause —
into obscurity, sacrifice, fierce joy.
Not merely into belief —
into the living, breathing Covenant Path.

The Rabbi still walks.
His dust still rises.
And He still calls:

"Come. Walk so close that My dust marks your life forever."

Will you?

MODERN APPLICATION AND REFLECTION: WHEN THE DUST SPEAKS

Have We Lost the Covenant of Dust?

We live in a generation that fears dust.

- We fear inconvenience.
- We fear disruption.
- We fear the visible evidence that following the Rabbi means following Him into discomfort, sacrifice, and surrender.

Somewhere along the way, Christianity in many places exchanged the dust of the Rabbi for the polished floors of cultural acceptance. And in doing so, we lost something sacred:

- **The proof of our belonging.**
- **The outward sign that we are not our own.**
- **The visible dustprints of covenant loyalty.**

Modern Dustlessness: The Hidden Drift

Hebraic discipleship demands *devekut* — clinging so closely to the Rabbi that separation feels like death. But modern faith often nurtures:

- **Casual association**, not covenant allegiance.
- **Observation**, not embodiment.
- **Occasional admiration**, not daily obedience.

Just as Israel repeatedly drifted from covenant love into comfortable compromise (Jeremiah 2:2–13), so too today we are tempted to walk a safer, sanitized path — far from the dust. **But a faith that remains clean remains distant.**

<u>*Signs You Are Walking Without Dust*</u>

Ask yourself:

- **Is my faith visible in sacrifice, or hidden behind convenience?**
- **Have I structured my life around following Jesus, or merely invited Him into my pre-structured life?**
- **Am I close enough to the Rabbi that His teachings interrupt my comfort?**

When prayer becomes a formality,
when obedience becomes negotiable,
when the Cross is admired but not carried,
the dust has been lost.

Dust was never accidental.
It was covenantal.

<u>*Restoring the Ancient Dust: Returning to Covenant Closeness*</u>

If dust is missing from your life, the solution is not guilt — it is movement. The Covenant Path calls you back:

- **Back to the proximity of His footsteps.**
- **Back to the hunger for His voice.**
- **Back to the wild, wonderful cost of daily surrender.**

Just as Israel had to **return** (*shuv*, שׁוּב) — to turn again toward the Covenant after every season of drift — so must we. Returning is not shame. Returning is the heartbeat of covenant love.

PRACTICAL PATHWAYS FOR GATHERING THE DUST AGAIN

1. Choose Daily Proximity Over Occasional Attendance

Discipleship is daily. It is rising each morning and asking:

"Rabbi, where are You walking today — and how can I stay close?"

- It means prioritizing His Word not as information, but as **invitation**.
- It means arranging your time, your work, your dreams around His presence, not your preferences.

✎ *Reflection:* What daily habits need to change so that your life orbits His path, not yours?

2. Choose Embodiment Over Admiration

In Hebraic tradition, a disciple was expected to **embody** the halakhah — to live the interpretation, not merely memorize it.

Today, the call remains:

- Forgive visibly.
- Serve invisibly.
- Walk humbly when pride tempts.
- Choose the narrow gate when broad doors open wide.

✎ *Reflection:* Where in your daily life can you embody the character of the Rabbi more visibly this week?

3. Choose Dust Over Safety

The disciple who gathers dust is the one who walks into places of:

- Need.
- Pain.
- Injustice.
- Hidden, costly obedience.

> If your path never costs you anything,
> if your sandals remain clean week after week,
> the question must be asked:

> *"Whose path am I truly following?"*

Reflection: Where is Jesus asking you to risk discomfort for the sake of covenant faithfulness today?

<u>*Small Group Reflection Questions*</u>

1. **Where do modern cultural values most tempt you to follow Jesus at a distance?**
2. **What daily rhythms could help you walk more closely behind the Rabbi?**
3. **What specific step of obedience would likely leave "dust" on your life this week?**
4. **How can your small group or family become a "community of the dust" together?**

<u>*A Modern Dust Story: Remembering the Ancient Road*</u>

Consider Leah:

Leah lived in a world of perfect images. Her faith was public — polished social media quotes, smiling Bible study selfies. But one day, she realized:

- She had spent more time curating her image of following the Rabbi than actually following Him.

When the Spirit whispered an invitation — to leave a prestigious position and step into hidden, thankless service among refugees — Leah hesitated. She loved Jesus in theory. But His footsteps were leading into uncomfortable territory.

She chose to walk.

She left behind applause.

She gathered dust.

And she found the Rabbi closer than she had ever imagined — laughing, weeping, walking among the broken.

Dust was not loss. It was life.

COVENANT CHALLENGE

The Covenant Path has never been paved with ease. It is marked by those willing to be covered in dust — the dust of surrender, the dust of obedience, the dust of relentless love.

Today the Rabbi calls:

"Come. Not partway. Not comfortably. All the way. Step close enough that My dust becomes your clothing."

Will you walk where sandals blister, where dreams die, where hope resurrects?

Will you walk close enough that the dust of your Rabbi marks you forever?

The dust is rising.

Will you?

COME AND SEE

RESPONDING TO THE INVITATION OF DISCIPLESHIP

"Come, and you will see."

— JOHN 1:39 (NIV)

THE AIR IN BETHANY WAS HEAVY WITH THE SCENT OF OIL AND baked bread, yet it carried another fragrance — something stirring in the hearts of those willing to hear it.

Andrew and another disciple stood in the lingering dust, watching the teacher whom John had declared "the Lamb of God." Curiosity burned in their chests. What kind of Rabbi walked without a crowd, without a title, without the polished authority of Jerusalem's finest?

When Jesus turned to face them, there was no rebuke, no suspicious inquiry. Just a simple, earth-shaking question:

"What do you seek?"

And then an invitation:

"**Come and see.**"

— JOHN 1:39

Two thousand years later, the dust of that invitation still hangs in the air — waiting for disciples who will hear it not as a suggestion, but as a summons to abandon life as they know it.

CORE TEACHING: COVENANT INVITATION

A Rabbi's Invitation Was Covenant, Not Casual

In the ancient Jewish world, every Rabbi carried authority, but few extended invitations lightly. Choosing disciples (*talmidim*) was not about gathering fans — it was about **entrusting covenant truth** to those willing to reorder their lives completely.

When Jesus said:

"**Come, follow Me**"

— MATTHEW 4:19

and later:

"**Come and see**",

— JOHN 1:39

He spoke in covenantal language deeply familiar to first-century Jews.

- In the Hebraic mindset, **movement symbolized acceptance**.
- To step after the Rabbi meant binding yourself to his life, teaching, and suffering.

Delaying was itself a form of rejection.
Movement was an act of loyalty.

"Come and See" Echoes the Ancient Covenant Pattern

Throughout the Scriptures, covenant moments demanded response:

- **Abraham** heard God's call to *"Go"* (Genesis 12:1) — and went without delay.
- **Moses** saw the burning bush (Exodus 3:2–4) — and turned aside to approach.
- **Isaiah** encountered God's throne (Isaiah 6:8) — and immediately said, *"Here am I; send me."*

Each covenant summons included:

- **An unexpected encounter** with the living God.
- **An invitation** to step away from the known into divine mystery.

- **A life-altering call** that demanded immediate trust and movement.

Discipleship under Jesus *is not a new path.*

It is a return to this ancient way — stepping at once toward the voice that speaks from holy ground.

Hebraic Thought: Movement Means Covenant Acceptance

In Hebraic culture, faith is never static.

- The very word *emunah* (אֱמוּנָה), often translated "faith," implies steadfastness in motion — loyalty proven over time, not merely belief held in thought.
- *Halakhah* (הֲלָכָה) — literally "the walking" — is the Jewish word for living faithfully under Torah.

Thus, when Jesus says "**Come**," He expects more than acknowledgment — He expects **movement born from trust**.

Come and See: Entering the Rabbi's Covenant Yoke

In Matthew 11:28–30, Jesus describes His yoke (*ol*, עוֹל):

"Take my yoke upon you and learn from me... For my yoke is easy and my burden is light."

In ancient Judaism, taking a Rabbi's yoke meant:

- Submitting to His authority.

- Trusting His interpretation of Scripture over your own instincts.
- Accepting the discipline and grace of becoming like Him.

The same is true today.

When we hear Jesus' *"Come and see,"* He is offering not only revelation, but responsibility — an opportunity to shoulder His life-shaping covenant.

Midrash Echo: Drawing Near with Steps

In Midrash Tehillim on Psalm 18:26, the sages taught:

"If you move toward Me even a handbreadth, I will move toward you by an arm's length."

Discipleship has always been initiated by God — but it demands that we respond with steps, not just sentiment.

The first disciples moved toward Jesus — and in doing so, entered the dustprint of a Kingdom that would overturn the world.

Refusing to Move: A Tragic Pattern

Throughout Israel's history, God lamented when His people hesitated:

- **Jeremiah 6:16** — *"But you said, 'We will not walk in it.'"*
- **Isaiah 30:15** — *"In repentance and rest is your salvation, but you would have none of it."*

Every generation faces the same decision:

- To **come and see,**
- or to **stay and wonder what might have been.**

Discipleship requires crossing the threshold of comfort into the dust of covenant.

The Rabbi still calls.

The road still waits.

Will we move?

MODERN APPLICATION AND REFLECTION: ANSWERING THE ANCIENT CALL

Why Our Feet Remain Still

Modern discipleship often stops short of movement:
- We admire the Rabbi.
- We discuss the Rabbi.
- We post quotes from the Rabbi.

But we resist walking behind Him into the costly places.

In truth, many today want the benefits of association without the cost of allegiance.

Yet covenant requires steps.

It always has.

Modern Barriers to Movement

1. **Fear of the Unknown**
   - "Where will He lead me?"
   - "What if the way is harder than I can bear?"

2. **Idolatry of Comfort**
    - "I'll follow — *but only if it enhances my plans.*"
    - "I'll come — *but not if it demands too much.*"
3. **Cultural Misformation**
    - "Following Jesus should feel easy."
    - "If it's difficult, maybe it isn't God's will."

Such thinking stands in direct contrast to the covenant invitation Jesus offers.

<u>*How to Step onto the Covenant Path Again*</u>

1. **Immediate Obedience**

Delaying obedience dulls the ears and stiffens the feet.When the Rabbi calls, the time to move is now.

Reflection: What has Jesus asked you to step into that you have delayed?

2. **Trust Without a Map**

The early disciples followed without GPS, strategic plans, or five-year projections. They trusted the Rabbi — and trusted the dust would prove enough.

Reflection: Where is Jesus asking you to trust the road more than the visible destination?

3. **Embrace Transformation Over Understanding**

Discipleship is first an act of covenant love, not intellectual mastery.

Reflection: What changes in you when you walk for love, not certainty?

<u>*Small Group Reflection Questions*</u>

1. What modern cultural lies make it hardest for you to answer Jesus' call quickly?
2. Where is fear hindering your movement?
3. What one step today would mark your return to walking closely behind the Rabbi?

COVENANT CHALLENGE

The dust rises where the Rabbi walks.

His voice still calls across oceans and centuries:

"Come and see. Come and walk. Come and become dust-covered proof that you belong to Me."

The choice is before you.
Step.
Or stay.

BEARING THE YOKE

ACCEPTING THE TEACHING AND
AUTHORITY OF THE RABBI

"Take my yoke upon you and learn from me, for I am gentle and humble in heart, and you will find rest for your souls."

— MATTHEW 11:29 (NIV)

SETTING THE SCENE: THE WORLD OF THE RABBI

THE MORNING SUN SHIMMERED ACROSS THE GALILEAN fields. Two oxen strained under the worn wood of a farmer's yoke — their necks bowed, their steps synchronized by discipline and unseen trust.

In the ancient world, to bear a yoke was to **accept authority** and **submit strength to purpose**. Younger oxen were often yoked alongside seasoned ones — not simply to pull weight, but to learn the steady cadence of obedience.

When a Rabbi invited a disciple to "take up his yoke," it

was an invitation to **surrender autonomy** — to entrust one's steps to the cadence of the Master.

When Jesus said:

"Take My yoke upon you and learn from Me..."

— MATTHEW 11:29

He wasn't offering rest from effort.

He was offering covenant rest — **the rest that only comes from surrendered strength.**

CORE TEACHING: COVENANT STRENGTH SURRENDERED

The Yoke in Hebraic Thought: A Mark of Covenant

In the Torah, the yoke (*ol*, עוֹל) symbolized covenant obligation.

- **Deuteronomy 28:48** warns of foreign yokes (oppression due to covenant disobedience).
- **Jeremiah 2:20** speaks of Israel "breaking off the yoke" in rebellion against God.
- Rabbinic tradition often referred to "the yoke of the Kingdom of Heaven" (*ol malchut shamayim*, עוֹל מַלְכוּת שָׁמַיִם) — willingly submitting to God's kingship.

Thus, a yoke was never viewed as a burden for the weary. It was an honor — a **visible, covenantal act of loyalty and alignment**.

When Jesus called weary hearts to take up His yoke, He was offering **not escape from weight, but exchange**:

- **Their crushing yokes** of sin, shame, and self-determination
- **For His covenant yoke** of mercy, grace, and obedience

<u>Jesus: The Gentle Rabbi Offering a New Yoke</u>

Jesus describes Himself uniquely:

"For I am gentle and humble in heart."

— MATTHEW 11:29

Unlike some legalistic Rabbis who burdened followers with hundreds of added regulations (cf. Matthew 23:4), Jesus' yoke restored covenant to its **relational essence**:

- Love the Lord your God (Deuteronomy 6:5 — *Shema* foundation).
- Love your neighbor as yourself (Leviticus 19:18).

Upon these two principles hung all Torah (Matthew 22:37–40). To walk in His yoke meant walking in covenant love — daily, visibly, sacrificially. It meant learning from the Rabbi not merely **what to believe**, but **how to walk, how to serve, how to surrender strength without losing joy**.

Midrash Insights: Learning from the Yoked Ones

Midrash Rabbah (Song of Songs 1:9) compares the faithful to "swift, yoked horses" — steady, beautiful in obedience, powerful not because of unbridled energy but because of coordinated trust. The faithful disciple:

- Moves in harmony with the Rabbi's steps.
- Bears the pace of grace rather than striving.
- Carries burdens that sanctify rather than crush.

Bearing the yoke is not weakness. It is **channeled covenant strength** — power placed fully under the authority of the Rabbi's hand.

Biblical Layers of Bearing the Yoke

- **Lamentations 3:27:** *"It is good for a man that he bear the yoke in his youth."*
  - Discipleship is most fruitful when covenant surrender begins early — before pride hardens the soul.
- **Galatians 5:1:** *"Do not submit again to a yoke of slavery."*
  - The new covenant yoke in Christ is not legalism, but freedom through Spirit-empowered obedience.
- **Philippians 2:5–8:**
  - Christ Himself bore the ultimate yoke — emptying Himself, humbling Himself to death, even death on a cross.

The covenant yoke does not enslave.
It liberates.

It does not crush.
It aligns.
It does not humiliate.
It sanctifies.

Covenant Discipleship: Yoked Hearts and Steady Feet

Taking up Jesus' yoke means:

- **Relinquishing rights** to self-centered dreams.
- **Accepting the disciplines** that shape true strength.
- **Learning obedience** through suffering, as even the Son did (Hebrews 5:8).

It means allowing your life to be harnessed to the Rabbi's pace, where ambition bows to service, where strength bends toward mercy, where every footstep becomes a covenant act of loyalty.

The ancient yoke is being offered anew.

The Rabbi waits.

Will you kneel your neck to covenant?

REFLECTION: LIVING UNDER THE RABBI'S YOKE

Why We Resist the Yoke

Today's culture teaches:

- **Autonomy is strength.**
- **Independence is virtue.**
- **Self-actualization is freedom.**

But the ancient Way — the Covenant Path — insists:

- True freedom is found in **yoked surrender**.
- True strength is discovered in **submission to love's commands**.

We resist the yoke because it requires:

- Trust over control.
- Humility over pride.
- Service over self.

Modern False Yokes

1. **The Yoke of Personal Achievement**
   - • Striving to prove worth through accomplishments.
   - • Exhaustion mistaken for spiritual maturity.
2. **The Yoke of Approval**
   - Living for the affirmation of others.
   - Allowing the crowd's opinion to guide obedience rather than the Rabbi's voice.
3. **The Yoke of Fear**
   - Refusing steps of faith because the outcome feels uncertain.
   - Choosing safety over sacrificial love.

These yokes are heavier than the one the Rabbi offers. And they leave souls crushed, not crowned.

How to Take Up the True Yoke Again

1. **Kneel First**

- The disciple's posture is downward — not scrambling for crowns, but kneeling to receive the yoke of Christ.

Reflection: Where does pride still resist the gentle hand of the Rabbi on your life?

2. Move at the Rabbi's Pace

- Do not run ahead.
- Do not fall behind.

The yoke ensures **closeness and cadence** — it is the slow, steady rhythm of covenant loyalty.

Reflection: Are you moving at the Rabbi's pace — or forcing your own speed?

3. Trust the Journey, Not Just the Destination

- The disciple does not demand a map.
- He trusts the Rabbi's direction, step by step.

Reflection: Where do you need to lay down your demand for clarity and walk by covenant trust?

<u>Small Group Reflection Questions</u>

1. What false yokes have you carried in recent seasons?
2. How has resistance to surrender stolen your joy?
3. What would it look like to fully accept Jesus' yoke this week — in visible, specific ways?

COVENANT CHALLENGE

The Master bends low, yoke in hand.
Not to oppress you, *but to free you.*
Not to shame you, *but to sanctify you.*

"Take My yoke upon you. Learn from Me. Walk with Me."

Will you bow your neck in covenant love?
Or will you keep striving under burdens never meant
for you?

The yoke is ready.
The dust rises.
The Rabbi calls.

Will you kneel?

HONOR AND SHAME

THE COMMUNAL FRAMEWORK FOR FOLLOWING WELL

"The wise inherit honor, but fools get only shame."

— PROVERBS 3:35 (NIV)

SETTING THE SCENE: THE WORLD OF THE RABBI

THE SUN BAKED THE NARROW STREETS OF CAPERNAUM, AND every set of eyes carried silent expectations. In the ancient world of Israel, **honor and shame were currencies more valuable than gold**.

A family's standing in the community, a man's ability to marry well, a Rabbi's influence — all were shaped by the invisible weight of communal honor. Every action added to or diminished your reputation. To be associated with shame was to be **exiled from belonging**.

When Jesus healed on the Sabbath, touched lepers, and spoke with Samaritans and tax collectors, He willingly crossed the honor boundaries of His world — and invited His disciples to do the same.

Following the Rabbi would mean bearing not only His dust, but **His shame** — and finding in that shame, the truest honor.

CORE TEACHING: COVENANT LOYALTY BEYOND REPUTATION

The Honor/Shame Culture of First-Century Israel

In first-century Jewish society:

- Honor was **public affirmation of worth**.
- Shame was **public disgrace, often permanent**.

Honor could be gained by:

- Faithfulness to Torah.
- Public piety.
- Right associations with respectable families and Rabbis.

Shame could be incurred by:

- Association with sinners.
- Rebellion against tradition.
- Visible failure in loyalty to God and community.

This cultural framework was not peripheral — it **shaped every relational and religious decision.**

Jesus: The Rabbi Who Embraced Redemptive Shame

Jesus systematically violated the honor codes of His time:

- He **touched the untouchable** (Mark 1:40–45).
- He **dined with tax collectors and prostitutes** (Luke 5:27–32).
- He **spoke publicly with women** (John 4:7–26).
- He **healed on forbidden days** (John 5:16).

Rather than guarding His social reputation, Jesus **wore shame like a mantle** — transforming it into the new standard of covenant loyalty.

When Isaiah prophesied the suffering Servant:

"He was despised and rejected by men, a man of sorrows and acquainted with grief..."

— ISAIAH 53:3

---

he described the path Jesus would walk — and the path His disciples would be invited to follow.

Hebraic Covenant Loyalty: A Test of Honor

In Hebraic thought, loyalty (*chesed*, חֶסֶד) was more valuable than external honor.

- Ruth clung to Naomi despite the shame of widowhood (Ruth 1:16–17).
- David honored Saul even when Saul hunted him (1 Samuel 24).

- Covenant loyalty was proven **not when it preserved reputation, but when it endangered it.**

Jesus' disciples were called to reframe honor:

- Not measured by community applause.
- Not secured through safe religious alliances.
- But grounded in **faithful proximity to the Rabbi,** no matter how much shame the world hurled at them.

Biblical Layers of Covenant Honor

- **Matthew 5:11–12:** *"Blessed are you when others revile you and persecute you... for so they persecuted the prophets who were before you."*
- **Romans 8:17:** *"If we are children, then we are heirs — heirs of God and co-heirs with Christ, if indeed we share in His sufferings..."*
- **Hebrews 13:13:** *"Let us, then, go to Him outside the camp, bearing the disgrace He bore."*

Following Jesus has always been a call to **bear honor through shame.** It is covenant fidelity tested in the fires of misunderstanding, accusation, and rejection.

Midrash Insight: The Weight of True Honor

The Talmud teaches:

"He who is shamed and does not shame back... upon him the Shechinah rests."

— GITTIN 36B

To absorb shame without retaliation was considered an act of supreme covenant loyalty — an echo of God's own patient mercy.

Thus, discipleship to Jesus requires:

- The surrender of managing our public image.
- The courage to be misunderstood for righteousness' sake.
- The joy of walking close enough to the Rabbi to wear His dust — and His disgrace.

REFLECTION: RECLAIMING COVENANT HONOR TODAY

The Modern Idol of Reputation

We live in a culture obsessed with image:

- Curated social media profiles.
- Self-promotion disguised as testimony.
- Pursuit of success sanitized from suffering.

Yet the call of the Covenant Path remains unchanged:

- Honor is found not in applause, but in loyalty to the King.
- True honor is measured by proximity to the dust and disgrace of the Rabbi's road.

Why We Fear Shame

1. **Loss of Status**

We fear being marginalized for convictions that contradict the culture.

2. **Loss of Influence**

We fear that visible association with "unpopular" teachings of Christ will cost us opportunities.

3. **Loss of Safety**

We fear that walking too closely behind the Rabbi will make us targets — for criticism, exclusion, or worse.

But Jesus warned clearly:

"If they persecuted Me, they will also persecute you."

— JOHN 15:20

Honor with God often costs honor with man.

How to Bear Redemptive Shame Well

1. **Anchor Identity in the Covenant**

You are not primarily a citizen of any earthly nation or a member of any social class. You are a *talmid* — a disciple bearing the mark of covenant belonging.

Reflection: Where have you allowed fear of public opinion to quiet your witness?

2. **Rejoice in Shared Suffering**

The early disciples left beatings "rejoicing that they were counted worthy to suffer dishonor for the Name" (Acts 5:41).

Reflection: How can you reframe shameful experiences as covenant honors?

3. **Walk Outside the Camp**

True disciples are willing to walk outside accepted systems — to bear the disgrace of standing where Jesus stands.

Reflection: Where is Jesus inviting you to "step outside the camp" and stand with Him?

Small Group Reflection Questions

1. Where have you been tempted to protect your reputation more than your loyalty to Christ?
2. What relationships or opportunities might you risk if you walk fully in covenant honor?
3. How can your community encourage one another to rejoice in sharing the Rabbi's disgrace?

COVENANT CHALLENGE

Honor is not found where the crowds cheer. It is found on the dusty paths where few are willing to walk — where loyalty shines brighter than popularity, where covenant outweighs convenience.

"Come. Bear My Name. Bear My dust. Bear My disgrace. And inherit My glory."

The Rabbi stands outside the camp, waiting. Will you step into the dust and shame of the Kingdom that cannot be shaken?

SITTING AT HIS FEET

HOW LEARNING IN JEWISH CULTURE INVOLVED ACTION

"Mary... sat at the Lord's feet listening to what he said."

— LUKE 10:39 (NIV)

SETTING THE SCENE: THE WORLD OF THE RABBI

THE HOME IN BETHANY WAS SMALL, BUT THE PRESENCE INSIDE was vast. The Rabbi sat, speaking not as a distant scholar, but as one who carried the living breath of Torah in His voice.

At His feet knelt Mary — abandoning her duties, ignoring cultural expectations, risking the shame of misplaced priorities. Around her, whispers grew.

"Shouldn't she be helping?"

"Shouldn't she know her place?"

But she stayed — silent, still, surrendered.

At the feet of her Rabbi, dust clinging to her garments, Mary found the only posture that mattered: **not standing in performance, but sitting in devotion.**

The dust of His teaching became her inheritance.

CORE TEACHING: CHOOSING PRESENCE OVER PERFORMANCE

Sitting at a Rabbi's Feet: A Posture of Covenant Devotion

In the first-century Jewish world:

- To sit at a Rabbi's feet was the formal position of a disciple (*talmid*).
- It signified **submission, loyalty, and covenant hunger** for wisdom.

Paul describes his own early training this way:

"I am a Jew, born in Tarsus of Cilicia, but brought up in this city. I studied under Gamaliel..."

— ACTS 22:3

Literally:

"I sat at the feet of Gamaliel."

To sit was to:

- Yield your will to the master's teaching.
- Restructure your life around his words.
- Accept transformation by proximity, not performance.

Mary of Bethany understood what many in her village did not: the true disciple does not impress — **the true disciple abides.**

Hebraic Layers: The Posture of Learning and Worship

In Hebraic thought:

- Learning is relational before it is informational.
- Wisdom is absorbed through reverence, not just intellect.

The Mishnah teaches:

"Anyone who sits in the presence of sages increases wisdom."

— AVOT 6:6

Thus, sitting was not passive — it was a **deliberate act of covenant pursuit.**

Mary's choice to sit:

- Defied cultural pressures toward busyness.
- Embodied the Shema's call: *"Love the Lord your God

with all your heart, soul, and strength" (Deuteronomy 6:5).

- Reaffirmed that discipleship begins not in action, but in **adoring reception**.

Jesus' Affirmation: The Better Portion

When Martha protested:

"Lord, do You not care that my sister has left me to serve alone?"

— LUKE 10:40

Jesus gently answered:

"Mary has chosen the good portion, which will not be taken away from her."

— LUKE 10:42

In Jewish tradition, "portion" (*chelq*, חֵלֶק) carried covenant significance:

- Israel's portion was the LORD Himself (Deuteronomy 32:9).
- The Levites' inheritance was not land, but the presence of God (Numbers 18:20).

Mary, by sitting at Jesus' feet, claimed her inheritance:

- Not the fleeting approval of performance.
- But the eternal treasure of proximity.

Biblical Layers: Presence Over Performance

- **Psalm 27:4:** *"One thing have I asked of the LORD... that I may dwell in the house of the LORD all the days of my life."*
- **John 15:4:** *"Abide in Me, and I in you."*
- **Revelation 3:20:** *"If anyone hears My voice and opens the door, I will come in and eat with that person, and they with Me."*

The invitation across Scripture is clear:

- Abide.
- Sit.
- Listen.
- Stay.

God values proximity over productivity.

Midrash Insight: Learning through Presence

The Midrash (Avot de-Rabbi Natan) tells us:

"A person learns most from his teacher's conduct rather than from his teachings."

Sitting close to the Rabbi shapes the soul not only

through words, but through the weight of His presence —
through the lived experience of covenant love.

The Discipleship of Sitting

Today, many rush to **do** for Jesus before they have **sat**
with Jesus. But Mary's example teaches:

- The disciple's strength flows from silence before it
  overflows into service.
- Covenant loyalty begins in being, not doing.
- Dust gathers best when our knees are bent low in
  worship.

REFLECTION: CHOOSING THE BETTER PORTION TODAY

The Modern Crisis of Busyness

We live in a culture that glorifies:

- Multitasking.
- Hustle.
- Constant visible productivity.

The world measures success by **output**.
But Jesus measures covenant loyalty by **presence**.
He still calls disciples not first to build, but to behold.
Not first to run, but to remain.

<u>Why We Resist Sitting</u>

1. **Fear of Invisibility**
   - If we sit at His feet, who will see us?
   - Who will applaud our worth?
2. **Addiction to Achievement**
   - We falsely believe we earn the Rabbi's love by completing more tasks.
   - We live under the crushing burden of "enoughness" instead of covenant belonging.
3. **Fear of Exposure**
   - Sitting still means facing the silence where fears, doubts, and hidden idols surface.

But only in the silence can the Rabbi heal what busyness hides.

<u>How to Return to the Rabbi's Feet</u>

1. **Prioritize Proximity Over Performance**

Block sacred time — unhurried, unproductive, deeply relational — to sit before God.

✍ *Reflection:* What would it cost you to guard daily time at the Rabbi's feet?

2. **Listen More Than Speak**

Prayer is not primarily informing God; it is being informed by Him.

✍ *Reflection:* What distractions most often steal your attentiveness to His voice?

3. **Value the Invisible Reward**

Heaven honors dust-stained garments more than polished resumes.

Reflection: How can you reframe "success" to match the Kingdom's standards this week?

<u>*Small Group Reflection Questions*</u>

1. How has busyness distorted your view of faithful discipleship?
2. Where do you need to sit more and strive less?
3. How can your community cultivate a rhythm of abiding presence together?

COVENANT CHALLENGE

The dust still gathers most richly where disciples kneel.

The Rabbi is still seated — still teaching, still welcoming, still forming the faithful in the hidden places.

He is not asking you first to perform.

He is asking you to stay.

To sit.

To listen.

To let the dust of His words mark your soul.

"Come. Sit at My feet. Choose the better portion. Let it never be taken from you."

Will you?

IMITATING THE TEACHER

BECOMING MIRRORS OF THE MASTER'S LIFE

"Everyone who is fully trained will be like their teacher."

— LUKE 6:40 (NIV)

SETTING THE SCENE: THE WORLD OF THE RABBI

THE AFTERNOON SUN BURNED LOW OVER THE FIELDS OF Galilee. Children played in the dust, echoing the gait and gestures of their fathers. It was instinct — this act of imitation.

In the ancient Jewish world, to **imitate** a respected elder, a Rabbi, or a father was seen as the highest form of honor. Disciples were not expected merely to **learn** from their Rabbi — they were expected to **become a living echo** of his life.

- Walk where he walked.
- Speak as he spoke.

- Pray as he prayed.
- Love what he loved.
- Rebuke what he rebuked.

Following Jesus, the true Rabbi, would require more than admiration. It would demand nothing less than full imitation — even when that road led to crosses, deserts, and empty tombs.

CORE TEACHING: BECOMING A LIVING ECHO

Discipleship in the Hebraic World: Imitation Over Information

In Hebraic tradition:

- A *talmid* (תלמיד) did not exist simply to **know** the Torah.
- A *talmid* existed to **embody** the way his Rabbi lived the Torah.

The Mishnah teaches:

"Be covered in the dust of their feet and drink in their words with thirst."

— AVOT 1:4

This imagery is not passive — it demands **movement**, **reflection**, and **replication**. The disciple's goal was to:

- Mirror the Rabbi's interpretations.
- Imitate the Rabbi's reactions.
- Internalize the Rabbi's relationship with God.

Discipleship was **not about independence**; it was about **covenant conformity** to the life of the one you followed.

<u>Jesus' Invitation: Not Simply to Believe, But to Become</u>

Jesus didn't call disciples simply to understand His teaching. He called them:

"Follow Me, and I will make you fishers of men."

— MATTHEW 4:19

The Greek word used here for "make" (*poieō*, ποιέω) suggests **transformation** — not simple instruction.

- **Paul** echoes this when he writes:

"Be imitators of me, as I am of Christ."

— 1 CORINTHIANS 11:1

- **John** reflects it when he teaches:

"Whoever claims to live in Him must live as Jesus did."

— 1 JOHN 2:6

True discipleship requires:

- Heart imitation (what the Rabbi values, the disciple values)
- Action imitation (what the Rabbi does, the disciple does)
- Sacrifice imitation (where the Rabbi goes, the disciple follows)

Hebraic Layers: To Walk Is To Transform

The Hebrew word *halakh* (הָלַךְ) — "to walk" — shapes the very concept of righteous living. Faith is never reduced to static belief. It is always embodied movement. Thus, disciples were judged not by what they said they believed, but by how they walked. This is why Jesus could say:

"By this everyone will know that you are My disciples, if you love one another."

— JOHN 13:35

Visible imitation is covenant proof.

Biblical Patterns of Imitation

- **Exodus 34:6–7:** God reveals His character — compassion, graciousness, slow to anger — and expects His people to reflect it.
- **Leviticus 19:2:** *"Be holy because I, the LORD your God, am holy."*
- **Ephesians 5:1:** *"Be imitators of God, as dearly loved children."*

Biblical faithfulness is always **imitational**:

- God sets the pattern.
- The people mirror it.

Midrash Insight: Emulation as Honor

In the Midrash (Tanchuma), it is said:

"Just as He is merciful, so you should be merciful. Just as He is gracious, so you should be gracious."

Imitation is worship. To walk like the Rabbi is to honor His teaching, His sacrifice, His heart.

The Disciple's Daily Covenant: Echo the Rabbi

Every day the disciple asks:

- Am I speaking like my Rabbi?
- Am I forgiving like my Rabbi?
- Am I resisting temptation like my Rabbi?

- Am I loving with my Rabbi's open, wounded
  heart?

Discipleship is not a destination. It is a daily act of covenant mimicry — a determined choice to let His dust settle on every part of our lives.

REFLECTION: LIVING AS A COVENANT REFLECTION

Why We Struggle to Imitate

Modern Christianity often teaches:

- Believe like Jesus.
- Admire Jesus.
- Represent Jesus.

But Scripture calls us:

- **Become like Jesus.**

The difference is covenantal. Imitation requires:

- Humility.
- Risk.
- The death of self-directed spirituality.

We hesitate to imitate because imitation costs visibility — it strips away autonomy, the ability to shape a life on our own terms.

<u>*False Models We Imitate Instead*</u>

1. **The Culture's Echo**
   - Mirroring success, fame, and power instead of compassion, humility, and sacrifice.
2. **The Comfortable Christian Image**
   - Building a respectable, moderate faith — without radical love or surrender.
3. **The Personal Dream**
   - Crafting a life based on individual fulfillment, with the Rabbi as occasional consultant.

True discipleship shatters false models. It insists on **total allegiance** to the Rabbi's path.

<u>*How to Return to Covenant Imitation*</u>

1. **See the Rabbi Clearly**

You cannot imitate what you do not see. Spend time absorbing the character of Jesus in Scripture — His mercy, His rebukes, His tears, His silences.

Reflection: What aspect of Jesus' character is most absent in your life right now?

2. **Choose Small Acts of Imitation Daily**
   - Forgive first.
   - Serve quietly.
   - Speak truth gently.
   - Stand faithfully under ridicule.

Every small echo builds a life that walks the Rabbi's path.

✒ *Reflection:* What small, hidden step of imitation could you take today?

3. **Embrace the Cross of Imitation**

Imitating the Rabbi means following Him into misunderstood places, costly love, and sacrificial hope.

✒ *Reflection:* Where is the Spirit inviting you to imitate the Rabbi even when it hurts?

Small Group Reflection Questions

1. Who or what are you most tempted to imitate other than Jesus?
2. How could you reorder your habits to better mirror the Rabbi's life?
3. What practical actions could your small group take this month to visibly echo Christ together?

COVENANT CHALLENGE

The dust rises behind the Rabbi still.
His hands still break bread.
His voice still calls sinners home.
His heart still pours out mercy on those the world would discard.

"Come. Walk after Me. Not merely in word, but in life. Echo Me until others no longer see you — only Me."

The ancient call of covenant imitation remains.

Will you?

THE COST OF THE CALL

LEAVING BEHIND SECURITY FOR KINGDOM PURPOSE

"Whoever wants to be my disciple must deny themselves and take up their cross and follow me."

— MATTHEW 16:24 (NIV)

SETTING THE SCENE: THE WORLD OF THE RABBI

THE SEA OF GALILEE shimmered under the weight of morning. Simon Peter bent over the familiar tang of fish-stained nets — the smell of provision, security, generational identity. Fishing was not merely an occupation. It was his **inheritance**, his **community standing**, his **lifeline**.

And then — a shadow on the water. A Rabbi, dusty from the road, wearing no formal badge of approval from Jerusalem's elite, spoke words that shattered the world Peter knew:

"Come, follow Me, and I will make you fishers of men."

— MATTHEW 4:19

Peter's fingers loosened their grip on the nets. In that moment, he was not just leaving a trade — he was surrendering a life.

Discipleship always costs something you think you cannot live without.

CORE TEACHING: COVENANT REQUIRES SURRENDER

Discipleship Was Covenant Departure

In ancient Israel, following a Rabbi meant more than adding religious learning to daily life. It demanded:

- Leaving the father's house (economic and social security).
- Leaving the village's honor (risking disgrace for missteps).
- Leaving predictable futures (surrendering inheritance rights).

Just as **Abraham** left Ur, walking into covenant trust

without a mapped future (Genesis 12:1–4), so every disciple left the known for the dust-filled unknown.

"By faith Abraham obeyed when he was called to go out... and he went out, not knowing where he was going."

— HEBREWS 11:8

Discipleship **was and is** a covenant act of courageous departure.

Jesus' Call: Not an Add-On, but a Total Reordering

Jesus' calls were always disruptive:

- **Matthew 8:19–22:** One disciple asks to bury his father first — Jesus replies, *"Let the dead bury their own dead."*
- **Luke 14:26–27:** *"If anyone comes to Me and does not hate father, mother, wife, children... yes, even their own life, such a person cannot be My disciple."*

In Hebraic hyperbole (intensified expression), "hate" meant **prioritize covenant loyalty so fiercely** that all other attachments dim by comparison.

Following the Rabbi demanded:

- New priorities.
- New allegiances.
- New definitions of success and belonging.

Hebraic Layers: Covenant Over Comfort

In Jewish covenant thinking:

- **Loyalty is proven through visible cost.**
- **Love is tested by action more than sentiment.**

The Mishnah teaches:

"No man truly learns unless he is willing to die for the words of the Torah."

— AVOT 6:6

If that was true for Torah learning, how much more for following the living Torah Himself — Jesus?

Biblical Patterns: The Cost of Covenant Walking

- **Moses** lost the palace of Egypt for the tents of the wilderness (Hebrews 11:24–26).
- **David** fled the royal courts into caves and wilderness (1 Samuel 22:1–2).
- **The Apostles** left trades, families, and freedom — most surrendered even their lives.

Discipleship always costs something precious. The Rabbi does not soften the call:

"Whoever wants to be My disciple must deny themselves and take up their cross daily and follow Me."

— LUKE 9:23

The way is dusty.
The way is costly.
The way is life.

Midrash Insight: Walking Beyond the Comfort Gates

The Midrash teaches:

"The righteous are recognized by the roads they travel."

— MIDRASH TEHILLIM ON PSALM 1:1

Where you walk reveals who your master is. If the cost of the Rabbi's call unsettles you, it is because it is meant to. Covenant was always a crossroads — where one path led to ease, and the other to eternal dustprints.

REFLECTION: PAYING THE PRICE TODAY

Why Modern Disciples Struggle with Cost

We have been conditioned to think:

- Faith should enhance comfort.
- Obedience should guarantee blessing.

- Following Jesus should align neatly with our personal dreams.

But the Covenant Path demands:

- Surrender of outcomes.
- Abandonment of idols.
- Sacrificial love even when it breaks our timelines.

The cost of the call is not fine print. It is written in the dust of the ancient road.

What the Call Costs Today

1. **Comfort**

You will be led into uncomfortable assignments — to love the unlovable, forgive the undeserving, trust through uncertainty.

2. **Reputation**

You will be misunderstood, slandered, rejected — sometimes by the very communities you once called home.

3. **Security**

You may be called to release jobs, homes, even lifelong dreams — to walk paths where the only safety is the Rabbi's nearness.

<u>*How to Embrace the Covenant Cost*</u>

1. **Acknowledge What You Must Leave**

Before Peter dropped his nets, he had to face what he was letting go.

✎ *Reflection:* What nets are you clinging to that the Rabbi is asking you to release?

2. **Count the Cost Joyfully**

Jesus said:

"Whoever does not carry their cross and follow Me cannot be My disciple."

— LUKE 14:27

The cross is not punishment. It is the door to covenant resurrection.

✎ *Reflection:* Where are you being invited to bear a cross today for the sake of deeper life?

3. **Trust the Worthiness of the Rabbi**

You are not surrendering to fate. You are surrendering to a living King who walks every dusty step beside you.

Reflection: How can you fix your eyes on the worth of the Rabbi when the cost feels heavy?

Small Group Reflection Questions

1. What comforts or securities make it hardest for you to follow Jesus fully?
2. Where are you negotiating with the Rabbi rather than surrendering?
3. How has someone else's costly obedience inspired your own faith journey?

COVENANT CHALLENGE

The call of the Rabbi is still costly. He still leads away from the comfortable crowds, toward hills called Calvary and gardens called Gethsemane.

He does not offer an easy road.

He offers Himself.

> *"Come. Drop your nets. Walk into the dust of surrender. Find the life that only the Covenant Path can give."*

Will you?

TRUSTING THE DUSTY PATH

DISCIPLESHIP AMIDST UNCERTAINTY
AND FEAR

---

*"Blessed are those whose strength is in you, whose hearts
are set on pilgrimage."*

— PSALM 84:5 (NIV)

SETTING THE SCENE: THE WORLD OF THE RABBI

THE WIND CARRIED FINE, STINGING DUST ACROSS THE ROAD TO
Jericho. The disciples pulled their garments tighter,
squinting through the swirl of dry air. The path ahead was
obscured — invisible in places where footsteps should have
been clear.

Still, the Rabbi walked forward, unwavering. He did not
slow when the dust thickened. He did not pause when the
landmarks disappeared. He trusted the path — because He
trusted the One who had sent Him. And He called His disciples to **trust the dust** — to keep walking when the road grew

uncertain, to follow even when clarity surrendered to covenant loyalty.

CORE TEACHING: COVENANT FAITH WALKS BEYOND SIGHT

Trust in Hebraic Thought: More Than Intellectual Assent

In Hebraic understanding:

- Trust (*batach*, בָּטַח) is not mere mental agreement.
- Trust is **bold reliance, secure dependence, covenantal rest** in action.

To trust is to:

- **Walk forward** before the road clears.
- **Step out** before assurances are visible.
- **Surrender control** without surrendering hope.

Trust (*batach*) implies **throwing oneself fully** onto the strength of another.

"Trust in the LORD with all your heart and lean not on your own understanding."

— PROVERBS 3:5

This was not theoretical to ancient Israel. It was survival — in deserts, in exiles, in battles, in barren places.

Trust was always the covenant call.

Jesus: The Rabbi Who Modeled Dusty Trust

Throughout His ministry, Jesus:

- Walked into towns knowing rejection awaited (Luke 4:24–30).
- Faced the uncertainty of betrayal and denial (John 13:21–30).
- Prayed under the crushing weight of Gethsemane's agony (Matthew 26:39).

And still He trusted:

- The Father's voice.
- The unseen plan.
- The Covenant that would not fail.

"Not My will, but Yours be done."

— LUKE 22:42

Jesus walked the dusty, uncertain path — not because it was clear, but because it was covenant.

Hebraic Layers: Trust as Movement

In Jewish teaching:

- **Faith is dynamic** — lived out through walking, serving, enduring.
- **True trust is proven** not when the way is smooth, but when it disappears into wilderness.

The Psalms echo this reality:

- **Psalm 23:** *"Even though I walk through the valley of the shadow of death, I will fear no evil, for You are with me."*
- **Psalm 84:5:** *"Blessed are those whose strength is in You, whose hearts are set on pilgrimage."*

The heart set on pilgrimage expects:

- Dust in the eyes.
- Thorn scratches on the arms.
- Winds that erase yesterday's footprints.

And still it moves forward.

Biblical Models of Dusty Trust

- **Abraham** leaving Ur, trusting in unseen promises (Genesis 12:1–4).
- **Joseph** enduring prison, trusting dreams long delayed (Genesis 39–41).
- **Ruth** walking dusty roads of widowhood and gleaning (Ruth 1–4).

- **Paul** planting churches through beatings,
  shipwrecks, and prisons (2 Corinthians 11:23–28).

Every covenant hero bore dust not only on their feet —
but woven into their souls.

Midrash Insight: Trust That Leaps

The Midrash teaches:

---

*"When Israel stood at the Red Sea, it was only after one man
leapt into the waters that the sea split."*

— MIDRASH TEHILLIM 114:1

Trust always leaps before the ground appears. Discipleship demands walking when the dust blinds. The Rabbi's
dust stings the eyes sometimes — but it also marks the
faithful who dared to keep walking.

REFLECTION: DUSTY TRUST IN OUR MODERN WILDERNESS

Why Modern Disciples Struggle to Trust the Dusty Path

We crave:

- GPS certainty.
- Strategic guarantees.

- Predictable outcomes.

But the Covenant Path is dusty — and dusty roads are sacred precisely because they require trust over clarity. Today's disciples often hesitate because:

- We confuse confusion with abandonment.
- We interpret silence as absence.
- We equate hardship with divine displeasure.

But the ancient way is different:

- Dust clouds are part of the journey.
- Wilderness seasons are not punishment but preparation.
- Silence is often the soil where faith takes deepest root.

Where Dusty Trust is Tested Today

1. **Vocational Uncertainty**
   - Trusting God when callings shift, doors close, opportunities evaporate.
2. **Relational Disappointments**
   - Trusting God's goodness when betrayal, loss, or loneliness crush expectations.
3. **Personal Wilderness**
   - Trusting God's presence when prayers seem unanswered and hope thins.

How to Walk the Dusty Road Well

1. **Hold Covenant Memory**

Remember the past faithfulness of the Rabbi.

- **Deuteronomy 8:2:** "*Remember how the LORD your God led you all the way in the wilderness these forty years.*"

✎ *Reflection:* What past dustprints of God's faithfulness can anchor you now?

2. **Speak Covenant Promises**

Dusty trust speaks promises louder than fears.

- **Psalm 42:5:** "*Why, my soul, are you downcast? Put your hope in God.*"

✎ *Reflection:* What covenant promise do you need to declare over your dust right now?

3. **Walk Anyway**

When the road disappears into haze, disciples keep walking. Not because they see the destination clearly — but because they trust the feet of the Rabbi they follow.

✎ *Reflection:* What is one step you can take this week despite the dust?

<u>Small Group Reflection Questions</u>

1. Where are you currently walking through a dusty, unclear path?
2.]What past moments of God's faithfulness can fuel trust now?
3. How can your small group encourage one another to walk faithfully even when the road is hidden?

COVENANT CHALLENGE

The dust still rises. The winds still obscure the trail sometimes. The promises sometimes seem slow in coming. But the Covenant Path remains.

And the Rabbi still walks —
steady, certain, sovereign —
even when you cannot see His footprints.

"Come. Trust Me beyond the clarity. Walk into the dust. Find the life hidden beyond the wilderness."

The call is ancient.
The road is sacred.
Will you trust the dust?

FOLLOWING THROUGH THE WILDERNESS

TRAINING GROUND FOR TRUST AND TRANSFORMATION

"Remember how the LORD your God led you all the way in the wilderness these forty years, to humble and test you in order to know what was in your heart."

— DEUTERONOMY 8:2 (NIV)

SETTING THE SCENE: THE WORLD OF THE RABBI

THE JUDEAN WILDERNESS STRETCHED VAST AND BRUTAL beyond the Jordan. Sun-scorched rock. Sparse thornbrush. Endless, winding paths swallowed by the silence of an unforgiving land.

The wilderness was not symbolic in ancient Israel. It was reality. A place where water was precious, direction treacherous, and survival uncertain.

It was here that Israel was tested.
It was here that David fled from kings and hid in caves.

It was here that John the Baptizer prepared the way.
It was here that Jesus Himself was driven — immediately
after His baptism (Mark 1:12).

No disciple is exempt from the wilderness. And it is often
in the wilderness that the dust on the feet becomes most
sacred.

CORE TEACHING: COVENANT ENDURANCE IN DRY PLACES

The Wilderness as Covenant Testing Ground

In Hebraic understanding, wilderness (*midbar*, מִדְבָּר) was
never seen as an accident. It was:

- A place of testing (Deuteronomy 8:2).
- A place of stripping away idols (Jeremiah 2:2–3).
- A place where covenant promises were both
  clarified and forged.

The wilderness revealed:

- Who truly trusted the Rabbi — and who only
  followed for provision.
- Who walked by sight — and who walked by
  covenant memory.

Jesus: Led by the Spirit into the Wilderness

Immediately after His baptism — the public affirmation of divine Sonship — Jesus was:

"...led by the Spirit into the wilderness to be tempted by the devil."

— MATTHEW 4:1

This was not a detour. It was covenant training. In the wilderness:

- Jesus faced hunger, temptation, isolation.
- Jesus refused shortcuts.
- Jesus clung to the written Word and the voice of His Father.

The true disciple's faith is not proven in crowds and celebrations. It is proven **where dust replaces feasts** and **the only songs are sung in solitude.**

Hebraic Layers: The Wilderness as Covenant Classroom

In Jewish thought:

- The wilderness (*midbar*) shares a linguistic root with *davar* (דָּבָר) — "word" or "speech."

Thus, the wilderness is:

- **The place where the Word is heard most clearly.**

- **The place where distractions are stripped away.**
- **The place where covenant fidelity deepens beyond feeling.**

Israel received the Torah not in cities of power, but in the silence of Sinai.

Biblical Patterns: Wilderness Always Precedes Inheritance

- **Israel** wandered for forty years before entering the Promised Land (Numbers 14:33–34).
- **David** fled into wilderness caves before ascending the throne (1 Samuel 22:1–2).
- **Elijah** stood atop Carmel only after a long desert journey (1 Kings 19).

Covenant faith is forged not on paved roads but in desert winds. The disciple must learn:

- **How to worship without immediate provision.**
- **How to trust when footsteps echo into emptiness.**
- **How to cling when the path ahead vanishes into barren hills.**

Midrash Insight: God's Presence in Desolation

The Midrash teaches:

"Wherever Israel wanders, the Shechinah goes with them."

— EXODUS RABBAH 15:20

The dust of wilderness is not proof of abandonment. It is proof of divine accompaniment. Even in the driest seasons, the Rabbi walks beside His disciples — sometimes unseen, but never absent.

REFLECTION: ENDURING WHEN THE WILDERNESS SEEMS ENDLESS

Why We Struggle in the Wilderness

Modern disciples often misunderstand wilderness seasons. We assume:

- God is punishing us.
- God has abandoned us.
- God is withholding blessing.

But the wilderness is **not a rejection**. It is **a refinement**. Just as precious metals are purified by fire, covenant loyalty is purified in the dry winds of perseverance.

Where Wilderness Testing Happens Today

1. **Delayed Dreams**
   - The callings we expected to blossom stall under barren skies.
2. **Hidden Faithfulness**
   - The unseen sacrifices, unnoticed obedience, unrewarded prayers.

3. **Silent Heavens**
   - The seasons when the Rabbi's voice feels distant, and our own steps sound deafeningly alone.

<u>*How to Walk Faithfully Through the Wilderness*</u>

1. **Remember the Dustprints Behind You**

Every wilderness pilgrim walks in ancient dustprints:

- Abraham's longing for an unseen inheritance.
- Moses' endurance without applause.
- Jesus' victorious resistance in the desert's silence.

🖊 *Reflection:* Whose dusty footsteps most inspire your perseverance right now?

2. **Feed on Covenant Memory**

The Word was Israel's survival bread.

- **Deuteronomy 8:3:** *"Man does not live on bread alone but on every word that comes from the mouth of the LORD."*

In dry seasons, disciples must eat the promises of Scripture as daily manna.

🖊 *Reflection:* What specific covenant promises must you feast on this week?

3. **Trust the God of the Dust**

Faith is not feeling. Faith is covenant commitment:

"I will follow, even when dust clouds the sun."

✎ *Reflection:* What step of stubborn covenant trust can you take today — even with dusty shoes and a weary heart?

Small Group Reflection Questions

1. Where do you currently feel you are walking through a wilderness?
2. How can remembering God's past faithfulness reshape your current perspective?
3. What practices can anchor you during seasons of dryness and silence?

COVENANT CHALLENGE

The desert winds still howl. The dust still blinds at times. The path still narrows into places where human strength dissolves. But the Covenant Path never disappears. And the Rabbi never leaves His own.

"Come. Follow Me through the dust. Endure beyond what you see. The wilderness is not the end — it is the beginning of deeper life."

Will you trust Him through the barren places?
Will you keep walking even when the dust hides the way?
The ancient road calls.
Step forward, disciple.

THE JOURNEY TO JERUSALEM

MOVING TOWARD THE CROSS ALONGSIDE JESUS

"As the time approached for him to be taken up to heaven, Jesus resolutely set out for Jerusalem."

— LUKE 9:51 (NIV)

SETTING THE SCENE: THE WORLD OF THE RABBI

THE ROAD TO JERUSALEM WOUND UPWARD — DUSTY, STEEP, and lined with memories of songs and sorrows. Every faithful Jew knew this journey. Three times a year they ascended to the Holy City (Exodus 23:17) — singing Psalms of Ascent, bearing offerings, longing to glimpse the splendor of Zion.

Jerusalem was **the heart of covenant hope** — the place where heaven and earth touched, where God's presence once rested in the Temple, where kings rose and prophets wept.

Now the Rabbi walked the same ancient road. But His

footsteps carried an urgency unknown even to the pilgrims of old. He walked not to celebrate — but to be broken.

The disciples followed, their feet stirring the dust of old songs, their hearts unknowingly stirring the dust of sacrifice.

CORE TEACHING: COVENANT DESTINY DEMANDS ASCENT

The Hebraic Meaning of Ascending to Jerusalem

In Hebrew, the word for going up to Jerusalem is **aliyah** (עֲלִיָּה) — meaning both a physical ascent and a spiritual elevation.

- Pilgrimage was not simply about geography.
- It was an act of covenant loyalty and longing.

Psalm 122:1 echoes this:

"I rejoiced with those who said to me, 'Let us go to the house of the LORD."

For ancient Israel:

- Jerusalem represented **covenant fulfillment**.
- The journey upward represented **heart movement toward God's purposes**.

Every step toward Jerusalem was a physical echo of an inner ascent — a rising of hope, loyalty, and sacrifice.

Jesus: The Rabbi Who Ascended to Surrender

Jesus' journey to Jerusalem was deeply covenantal:

- He walked not only to teach but to **fulfill the Torah and the Prophets** (Matthew 5:17).
- He moved with full knowledge that Jerusalem would crown Him with thorns, not gold (Luke 9:22).

Luke describes the pivotal moment:

"As the time approached for Him to be taken up to heaven, Jesus resolutely set out for Jerusalem."

— LUKE 9:51

Resolutely — literally, **He set His face like flint** (cf. Isaiah 50:7). The Rabbi did not drift toward destiny. He walked into it with **covenant determination**.

Hebraic Layers: Covenant Loyalty Over Comfort

In Jewish covenant tradition:

- Loyalty is proven not when the Temple celebrations are loud,
- But when the pilgrim walks upward under the weight of sacrifice.

Aliyah was costly:

- Travel was dangerous.
- Resources were stretched.
- Time was surrendered.

Yet covenant loyalty compelled the journey. Jesus' own ascent embodies this heart: an unwavering movement toward fulfilling the Father's plan, no matter how the crowds shifted or the road darkened.

Biblical Layers: The Path to Glory Is Paved with Suffering

- **Psalm 84:5–7:** *"Blessed are those whose strength is in You, whose hearts are set on pilgrimage... They go from strength to strength till each appears before God in Zion."*
- **John 12:23–24:** *"The hour has come for the Son of Man to be glorified... unless a kernel of wheat falls to the ground and dies, it remains only a single seed."*
- **Hebrews 12:2:** *"For the joy set before Him, He endured the cross, scorning its shame, and sat down at the right hand of the throne of God."*

Glory and suffering are intertwined in covenant ascent.

Midrash Insight: The Journey Reveals the Heart

The Midrash teaches:

"The true worshiper is not the one who arrives first, but the one who walks with a heart fully surrendered to the journey."

It is not speed but surrender that marks the disciple. It is not applause but persistence that proves covenant loyalty.

REFLECTION: WALKING OUR OWN JERUSALEM ROAD

Why Modern Disciples Struggle to Ascend

We live in a culture that celebrates:

- Instant gratification.
- Comfort without cost.
- Avoidance of suffering.

Yet the Covenant Path always ascends through sacrifice. Discipleship demands:

- Uphill roads.
- Narrow gates.
- Faithful steps when the city ahead glows with uncertainty, not guarantees.

Where Jerusalem Journeys Happen Today

1. **Costly Obedience**
   - Saying "yes" to callings that strip pride and security.

2. **Hidden Sacrifices**
   - Serving in unseen ways when others celebrate elsewhere.
3. **Persevering Love**
   - Continuing to forgive, serve, believe — even when love is not returned.

How to Keep Ascending When the Path Steepens

1. **Set Your Face Like Flint**

Strengthen your covenant resolve.

- **Isaiah 50:7:** *"Because the Sovereign LORD helps me, I will not be disgraced. Therefore have I set my face like flint."*

🖊 *Reflection:* Where do you need to renew your resolve to walk upward even when the road grows steep?

2. **Anchor in Covenant Joy**

Jesus endured not by gritting His teeth — but by fixing His eyes on covenant joy.

🖊 *Reflection:* What covenant promises can fuel your endurance this season?

3. **Walk for the Audience of One**

Jerusalem journeys are rarely celebrated by the crowds. The journey is for the Father's pleasure — not public approval.

Reflection: Whose approval are you most tempted to seek today?

<u>*Small Group Reflection Questions*</u>

1. Where is Jesus calling you to ascend toward hard obedience?
2. What small sacrifices are forging covenant faithfulness in you?
3. How can your group encourage one another to walk toward Jerusalem together?

COVENANT CHALLENGE

The climb still waits. The dust still rises. The path to covenant fulfillment still ascends steep, rocky hills. And the Rabbi still leads — His face set toward a Kingdom unseen by human eyes, His steps calling you upward into costly joy.

"Come. Set your face toward covenant destiny. Walk into Jerusalem. Walk into surrender. Walk into resurrection."

Will you?
The journey is not easy.
But it is sacred.

THE HIDDEN STRENGTH
(MEEKNESS)

STRENGTH THROUGH HUMILITY AND RESTRAINT

"Blessed are the meek, for they will inherit the earth."

— MATTHEW 5:5 (NIV)

SETTING THE SCENE: THE WORLD OF THE RABBI

A ROMAN SOLDIER SHOUTED AT THE ROADSIDE CROWD NEAR Capernaum. His voice cut through the wind — commanding, sharp, unquestioned.

But just beside the commotion stood the Rabbi. Calm. Silent. Still. He didn't clench His fists. He didn't assert His authority. He carried Himself with a quiet power — the kind of presence that unsettled without intimidation.

This Rabbi touched lepers. He dined with sinners. He refused to retaliate. And yet, storms obeyed His voice. Demons fled at His presence. Death surrendered at His command. This was **meekness** — not weakness, but strength

fully surrendered to the Father's will. And He invited His disciples to learn it, wear it, and walk it.

CORE TEACHING: MEEKNESS IS STRENGTH UNDER COVENANT CONTROL

Hebraic Understanding of Meekness: Anavah (עֲנָוָה)

In Hebraic tradition, *anavah* (meekness/humility) is not about insecurity or timidity. It is:

- Knowing your strength
- Submitting your strength
- Trusting God's timing, justice, and authority above your own

Moses was called:

"Very meek, more than all people who were on the face of the earth."

— NUMBERS 12:3, ESV

And yet Moses:

- Faced Pharaoh.
- Led millions through desert wilderness.
- Confronted idolatry with fiery covenant zeal.

Meekness did not diminish his leadership. It deepened it.

Jesus: The Rabbi of Meekness

Jesus described Himself with shocking vulnerability:

"Take My yoke upon you... for I am gentle and humble in heart."

— MATTHEW 11:29

He did not flaunt strength. He modeled surrender.

- He kept silent before Pilate (Mark 15:5)
- He wept over Jerusalem (Luke 19:41)
- He bent low to wash feet (John 13:5)
- He absorbed betrayal without retaliation

And yet:

- He calmed storms
- Rebuked false religion
- Carried the authority of heaven

Jesus showed us that **meekness is what divine strength looks like in covenantal hands.**

Hebraic Layers: Strength That Knows Its Source

In Jewish thought, **true strength** (*gevurah*, גְּבוּרָה) is always linked to self-mastery — not domination over others.

The Talmud teaches:

"Who is strong? One who conquers his own impulse."

— PIRKEI AVOT 4:1

This aligns perfectly with *anavah*:

- The disciple who knows who they are
- And refuses to exalt themselves apart from God's will

The meek disciple:

- Does not need to force respect
- Does not demand attention
- Is powerful precisely because they walk **under covenant authority**

Biblical Layers: Meekness as Kingdom Identity

- **Psalm 37:11:** *"The meek shall inherit the land and delight themselves in abundant peace."*
- **Matthew 5:5:** *"Blessed are the meek, for they shall inherit the earth."*
- **Philippians 2:5–8:** *"He humbled Himself by becoming obedient to the point of death, even death on a cross."*

The disciple who walks in meekness:

- Is aligned with heaven's character

- Is entrusted with heaven's influence
- Inherits kingdom authority through surrender, not striving

Midrash Insight: Power Clothed in Gentleness

The Midrash teaches:

"The Torah was given in fire, but it was carried by Moses in meekness."

Covenant truth is most trustworthy when carried in covenant character. The Rabbi's yoke is light because it is carried on the shoulders of the meek.

REFLECTION: LIVING WITH QUIET FIRE

Why Meekness is Misunderstood Today

Modern culture equates power with:

- Loudness
- Control
- Platform
- Charisma

But in the kingdom of God:

- Meekness is might

- Gentleness is authority
- Surrender is strength

We resist meekness because it feels like:

- Vulnerability
- Passivity
- Exposure

But Jesus showed us that **meekness is not the absence of strength — it is the refusal to wield it apart from love.**

Where Meekness is Needed Today

1. **In Leadership**
   - Leading with restraint
   - Listening before reacting
   - Serving quietly over performing loudly
2. **In Relationships**
   - Offering grace when others deserve rebuke
   - Choosing silence when ego demands a response
3. **In Ministry and Influence**
   - Trusting God's elevation over self-promotion
   - Lifting others before asserting self

How to Cultivate the Meekness of the Rabbi

1. **Practice Restraint**

Choose not to react when wronged — not out of fear, but out of trust in God's justice.

🖋 *Reflection:* Where is God asking you to release your right to "have the last word"?

2. Embrace Hiddenness

Let your value come from the Rabbi's affirmation, not public applause.

🖋 *Reflection:* What can you do in secret this week to bless someone without credit?

3. Surrender Strength Daily

Pray not for more power, but for deeper surrender.

🖋 *Reflection:*What area of strength in your life needs to be placed under the Rabbi's authority?

<u>*Small Group Reflection Questions*</u>

1. What assumptions have you carried about meekness that need to be unlearned?
2. How can you practice covenant gentleness in your most difficult relationships?
3. What does it look like for your group to become a "community of quiet strength"?

COVENANT CHALLENGE

The world needs fire, but fire under control. The Kingdom needs strength, but strength shaped by covenant love. The Rabbi still kneels to wash feet. He still entrusts His authority to the meek. He still invites disciples to carry crosses, not crowns.

"Come. Let your strength serve love. Let your power bow to grace. Let meekness mark you with My dust."

Will you?
The world may not notice.
But heaven will.

RABBI OF THE CROSS

RADICAL REDEFINITION OF LEADERSHIP AND GREATNESS

"For the message of the cross is foolishness to those who are perishing, but to us who are being saved it is the power of God."

— 1 CORINTHIANS 1:18 (NIV)

SETTING THE SCENE: THE WORLD OF THE RABBI

THE ROAD OUTSIDE THE CITY GATE WAS THICK WITH DUST AND dread. Passover crowds swelled the streets of Jerusalem, pilgrims celebrating liberation. But just outside — a hill shaped like a skull — the Rabbi was dying. Not in silence, but in shame.

He had washed feet, healed blind men, opened scrolls in synagogues. Now His hands were pierced, His teaching interrupted by jeers, His body stretched in disgrace. No Rabbi taught like this. No Messiah suffered like this. And yet this was the final classroom.

The Cross was not a detour — it was the **defining *halakhah* of His discipleship**. The Rabbi of the Cross was teaching love not just in words, but in blood.

CORE TEACHING: THE CROSS IS THE CURRICULUM

In Hebraic Terms: The Cross Was Curse and Covenant

Deuteronomy 21:23 declares:

"Anyone who is hung on a tree is under God's curse."

To die on a cross was to be:

- Shamed
- Cursed
- Forgotten

And yet Jesus — Israel's true King and final Rabbi — embraced this path willingly. He inverted the shame and redefined the curse.

Paul would later write:

"Christ redeemed us from the curse of the law by becoming a curse for us."

— GALATIANS 3:13

This was covenant loyalty — a Rabbi who **bore our shame so we could bear His righteousness**.

Jesus' Invitation to the Cross

Jesus never softens the ask. He teaches:

"If anyone would come after Me, let him deny himself and take up his cross daily and follow Me."

— LUKE 9:23

The *talmid* in the first century would follow his Rabbi even when the road led into danger. But Jesus' path doesn't just risk death — **it requires it**:

- Death to self-will
- Death to pride
- Death to the illusion that we can follow Jesus without surrender

The Cross is not a metaphor. It is **the entrance into covenant life**.

Hebraic Layers: Sacrifice as the Path to Covenant Renewal

Throughout Torah, covenant was sealed in blood:

- Abraham and the severed animals (Genesis 15)
- Passover lamb and the Exodus (Exodus 12)
- Yom Kippur sacrifices (Leviticus 16)

The disciple of Jesus learns that:

"Without the shedding of blood there is no forgiveness of sins."

— HEBREWS 9:22

But now — the blood is not from lambs. It is from the Rabbi.

"This is My blood of the covenant, poured out for many for the forgiveness of sins."

— MATTHEW 26:28

The Cross Is the Center of the Covenant Path

The Cross is not:

- A tragic end
- A temporary stop
- A dramatic symbol

It is the center. It is the *halakhah* — the *way* — of the Rabbi:

- Mercy in the face of injustice
- Love in the place of betrayal
- Surrender in the presence of power

Paul would later summarize discipleship this way:

"I have been crucified with Christ. It is no longer I who live, but Christ who lives in me."

— GALATIANS 2:20

Midrash Insight: The Cost of True Love

The sages said:

"Where there is no sacrifice, there is no true covenant."

The Cross reveals that Jesus was not only a teacher of the law — He was its fulfillment, its sacrifice, its human embodiment. And He calls His disciples not just to admire Him — but to follow.

To carry.

To die daily.

REFLECTION: CARRYING THE CROSS IN A COMFORTABLE WORLD

Why We Avoid the Cross

We prefer:

- Inspiration over imitation
- Belief over sacrifice
- Applause over suffering

But the Cross offends every comfort idol:

- It demands all.
- It humbles completely.
- It reveals that **covenant love costs blood and breath and pride.**

Today's disciples are tempted to:

- **Admire the crucifixion without being crucified**
- **Preach grace without surrendering autonomy**

But the Rabbi of the Cross is clear:

"No servant is greater than his master... If they persecuted Me, they will persecute you also."

— JOHN 15:20

<u>*Where the Cross Appears in Everyday Discipleship*</u>

1. **Forgiveness That Costs**

Choosing to forgive deep wounds — not once, but seventy times seven.

2. **Love Without Return**

Serving where there is no applause. Giving where there is no gratitude.

3. **Obedience When It Hurts**

Saying "yes" to God when it breaks your dream open like an alabaster jar.

<u>*How to Carry the Cross With the Rabbi*</u>

1. **Embrace the Death That Leads to Life**

Jesus said:

"Whoever loses his life for My sake will find it."

— MATTHEW 16:25

Every true disciple dies — not once, but **daily**.

✎ *Reflection:* What comfort, right, or desire must you place on the Cross this week?

2. **Don't Carry It Alone**

Even Jesus needed Simon of Cyrene (Luke 23:26). Discipleship is a covenant community carrying covenant weight — together.

Reflection: Who is helping you carry your cross — and whose burden are you sharing?

3. **Fix Your Eyes on the Rabbi**

The Cross was not the end. It was the gate to resurrection. The Cross is heavy, but the joy beyond it is weightier still.

Reflection: What resurrection hope fuels your willingness to carry the Cross?

Small Group Reflection Questions

1. What part of Jesus' crucifixion challenges you the most personally?
2. How is God calling you to "take up your cross" in your current season?
3. What joy lies on the other side of obedience that might strengthen you today?

COVENANT CHALLENGE

The Cross still casts its shadow over the dusty road.
  Not to intimidate.
  But to illuminate.

The Cross is where the old self ends and the covenant life begins. The Rabbi still walks that path — not in glory first, but in surrender.

"Come. Take up your cross. Walk behind Me. Lose your life, and find it hidden in Mine."

This is not metaphor. This is discipleship. This is covenant.

Will you carry the Cross?

BEARING THE RABBI'S AUTHORITY

PASSING ON THE COMMISSION TO DISCIPLE OTHERS

"All authority in heaven and on earth has been given to me. Therefore go and make disciples of all nations..."

— MATTHEW 28:18–19 (NIV)

SETTING THE SCENE: THE WORLD OF THE RABBI

THE CROWDS HAD SEEN TEACHERS BEFORE. THEY HAD HEARD voices explain the Torah. They had watched Rabbis debate Halakhah in village squares. But never like this.

"They were amazed at His teaching, because He taught them as one who had authority, not as the teachers of the law."

— MARK 1:22

This Rabbi didn't quote other Rabbis. He didn't ask permission to speak. He healed with a word. He silenced storms with a breath. **And then, shockingly, He entrusted that same authority to His disciples.**

Authority to speak.

To bind.

To loose.

To carry His mission — and bear His name.

Disciples do not only follow.

They carry.

And what they carry shapes everything.

CORE TEACHING: CARRYING COVENANT AUTHORITY FAITHFULLY

<u>*In Hebraic Culture: Shmikhah (Authority) Was Passed*</u>

In first-century Judaism, Rabbis taught with one of two levels of authority:

1. **Standard Rabbinic Teaching**
   - Based on quoting previous Rabbis
   - Limited to interpretation, not innovation
2. ***Shmikhah*** (סְמִיכָה) **— Exceptional Authority**
   - Recognized spiritual authority passed down
   - Empowered a Rabbi to issue new rulings or insights directly under divine guidance
   - Always passed from **two witnesses** (cf. Moses to Joshua — Numbers 27:18–23)

The people recognized that **Jesus taught with *shmikhah***

— unlike the scribes (Mark 1:22). He did not cite others. He spoke as **the Source**.

Jesus: The Rabbi Who Bestowed His Authority

Jesus didn't only walk in divine authority — He gave it away.

- **Luke 9:1–2:** *"He gave them power and authority to drive out all demons and to cure diseases... and He sent them out to proclaim the Kingdom."*
- **Matthew 28:18–20:** *"All authority in heaven and on earth has been given to Me. Therefore go..."*
- **John 20:21:** *"As the Father has sent Me, I am sending you."*

This is not casual delegation. It is covenant commissioning. Just as Rabbis would eventually commission disciples to carry their *halakhah*, Jesus sends His *talmidim* to carry His way — His dust, His teaching, and His **authority**.

Hebraic Layers: Authority as Stewardship, Not Status

In Jewish tradition:

- Authority is not seized — it is **entrusted**.
- Authority is not self-glorifying — it is **self-emptying**.

The Talmud teaches:

"He who seeks honor shall not find it, but he who flees honor — honor pursues him."

— PIRKEI AVOT 4:13

This perfectly echoes Jesus' model:

- Authority is carried **for others**, not over others.
- The one with the greatest authority **washes the most feet** (John 13:12–17).

Biblical Patterns of Carried Authority

- **Moses → Joshua:** Transference of Spirit and leadership (Deuteronomy 34:9)
- **Elijah → Elisha:** Double portion of prophetic mantle (2 Kings 2:9–10)
- **Jesus → The Twelve (and then the 72):** Sent ones, entrusted with message and power (Luke 10:1–3, 16)

Authority in Scripture is always:

- **Costly to carry**
- **Rooted in obedience**
- **Empowered by surrender**

Midrash Insight: The Weight of the Name

The sages taught:

"Whoever carries the Name must walk in the weight of its holiness."

Jesus sends His disciples **in His Name** — not as mere messengers, but as bearers of His very essence. To carry the Rabbi's authority is to:

- Speak with truth
- Serve with humility
- Walk with power — **but under covenant restraint**

REFLECTION: WALKING IN ENTRUSTED POWER

Why Authority Is Often Misused or Feared

Today's culture both idolizes and resents authority.

- Some abuse it — using spiritual power for control or self-gain.
- Others avoid it — equating leadership with pride.

But covenant disciples must walk a better path. **We carry the Rabbi's authority not for platform, but for service.**

- To bind what must be bound (Matthew 16:19)

- To loose what must be loosed
- To represent heaven's heart in earthly places

This is not **celebrity discipleship**. It is **commissioned responsibility**.

Where Authority is Needed Today

1. **In Prayer**

Disciples must intercede with boldness — not timid suggestions, but Kingdom declaration.

2. **In Truth-Telling**

Disciples must speak the Rabbi's truth, even when culture demands silence.

3. **In Service**

Disciples must use power to lift, not dominate. Jesus said:

"The greatest among you will be your servant."

— MATTHEW 23:11

How to Carry the Rabbi's Authority Faithfully

1. **Remember Whose Name You Bear**

You speak not in your strength, but in the authority of the Crucified and Risen One.

Reflection: Where have you forgotten the weight — and privilege — of carrying Jesus' Name?

2. **Speak What He Has Spoken**

Authority grows not from volume, but from alignment with His Word.

Reflection: Are your words rooted in Scripture and spoken from a surrendered heart?

3. **Walk With Gentle Boldness**

Disciples don't dominate — they represent.
They rebuke with tears.
They lead with towels.
They heal with pierced hands.

Reflection: Where is God calling you to lead boldly — but gently — in His authority?

Small Group Reflection Questions

1. How has your view of spiritual authority been shaped by good or poor examples?
2. What spiritual authority has Jesus entrusted to you that you've been afraid to walk in?
3. How can your group help one another walk in the Rabbi's authority with courage and humility?

COVENANT CHALLENGE

The Rabbi still entrusts His Name. He still sends disciples to speak, love, lead, and serve in His power. This is not a casual badge. It is a covenant burden — to walk as He walked, speak as He spoke, and carry His heart into every darkened place.

"Come. Bear My authority. Let your strength be My strength. Let your words be My words. Let the dust of My Name cling to your every step."

Will you walk in what He has entrusted?
Will you carry the Rabbi's authority?

A LEGACY OF DUSTPRINTS

BECOMING DISCIPLE-MAKERS ACROSS GENERATIONS

"The things you have heard me say in the presence of many witnesses entrust to reliable people who will also be qualified to teach others."

— 2 TIMOTHY 2:2 (NIV)

SETTING THE SCENE: THE WORLD OF THE RABBI

THE RABBI WAS GONE — BUT THE DUST STILL LINGERED. NOT the dust of despair, but of **continuity**. The kind that clings to sandals even after the feet have moved on. The kind that tells stories without speaking. The kind that marks the ground where love has walked.

The early disciples gathered, not to invent something new, but to **carry something forward**. They remembered His footsteps on Galilean roads. They echoed His words in upper rooms. They reenacted His sacrifices in their own. And soon, their own feet began to leave dustprints.

Not of fame — *but of faith.*
Not of power — *but of presence.*
Their lives became maps for those who would follow.

CORE TEACHING: DISCIPLESHIP WAS ALWAYS MEANT TO BE GENERATIONAL

In Hebraic Thought: Disciples Multiply by Imitation

The goal of every *talmid* was not just to become like the Rabbi — but to **pass on the Rabbi's way** to others.

Discipleship was never about self-fulfillment. It was about **transmission**. Moses trained Joshua. Elijah passed his mantle to Elisha. Jesus trained the Twelve — not only to follow Him, but to **build others** who would do the same (Matthew 28:18–20). This was not optional. It was **covenant expectation**.

"Teach them to obey everything I have commanded you."

Disciples leave trails — and those trails become the roads others walk.

The Dustprint as a Covenant Mark

In Hebraic tradition, dust had both symbolic and literal significance:

- **It marked where someone had walked.**

- **It told a story without words.**
- **It lingered longer than the moment.**

"Walk so close behind your Rabbi that the dust of his feet covers you."

— MISHNAH, AVOT 1:4

And if you walk long enough, **your own feet begin to leave dust behind** — visible proof that you did not just believe, you followed.

Biblical Layers: A Faith That Others Can Walk Behind

- **Psalm 78:6:** *"So the next generation would know, even the children yet to be born, and they in turn would tell their children."*
- **2 Timothy 2:2:** *"And what you have heard from me... entrust to reliable people who will also be qualified to teach others."*
- **Hebrews 13:7:** *"Remember your leaders, who spoke the word of God to you. Consider the outcome of their way of life and imitate their faith."*

Legacy is not accidental. It is **the natural byproduct of consistent covenant walking**. Dust that clings becomes dust that marks.

<u>Hebraic Layers: Remembering and Repeating the Way</u>

Jewish discipleship emphasizes:

- **Memory** (*zakar*, זָכַר) — not nostalgia, but covenant recall
- **Emulation** — walking as others walked
- **Transmission** — teaching sons and daughters not only beliefs, but lifestyle

The Shema commands:

"These commandments that I give you today are to be on your hearts. Impress them on your children..."

— DEUTERONOMY 6:6–7

Covenant dust is passed down intentionally. It is a **legacy of walking** — not only of words.

<u>Midrash Insight: The Echo of Footsteps</u>

The sages taught:

"Blessed is the disciple whose footsteps echo the master's, and whose dust guides the next."

True discipleship is not just about finishing well — but about **leaving a visible, walkable path** for those who come behind.

REFLECTION: LEAVING DUSTPRINTS THAT OUTLAST YOU

What Kind of Legacy Will You Leave?

Every day, you are leaving something behind. The only question is:

Will it lead anyone closer to the Rabbi?

Modern culture celebrates legacies of:

- Fame
- Achievement
- Accumulation

But the Kingdom celebrates **faithfulness**:

- Invisible obedience
- Sacrificial love
- Footsteps walked when no one applauded

Dustprints matter — because they **outlive your name.**

How Dustprints Are Left Today

1. **By Walking Consistently**
   - Following Jesus day after day — even in quiet seasons
   - Your habits shape others, even if you never speak

2. **By Speaking Truth in Love**
   - Your words become stepping stones for others
   - Your testimony becomes someone's map
3. **By Discipling Others Intentionally**
   - Sharing your journey
   - Inviting others into the dust

Reflection: Who is walking behind you — and what trail are you leaving?

Barriers to Leaving a Faithful Legacy

1. **Shame from the Past**
   - "My story is too broken."
   - → The Rabbi's dust redeems everything.
2. **Fear of Inadequacy**
   - "I'm not a teacher."
   - → You are a **witness**. You carry dust. That is enough.
3. **Distraction with the Present**
   - "I'll pour into others later."
   - → The best legacy is written in today's ordinary steps.

How to Leave Covenant Dustprints

1. **Walk in Public Obedience**: Let your devotion be visible — not performative, but real.

2. **Mentor Intentionally**: Who can you invite into your life — to learn by walking with you?

3. **Live a Life Worth Imitating**: Live so that, when others ask what it means to follow Jesus, someone

points to your life and says, "Walk where they walked — they followed the Rabbi well."

<u>*Small Group Reflection Questions*</u>

1. Who has left dustprints in your life — and how have they shaped you?
2. What trail is your life currently leaving for others to follow?
3. Who could you invest in intentionally this year?

COVENANT CHALLENGE

The dust on your feet was never just for you. It was meant to mark the road. To show the way. To create a path for the next disciple who dares to follow.

> ***"Come. Walk the Covenant Path. Leave a legacy of dust. Let your life be a map. Let your faith become a trail."***

The next disciple is watching.
Will you leave them a way to walk?

EPILOGUE: STILL IN THE DUST

"Stand at the crossroads and look; ask for the ancient paths, ask where the good way is, and walk in it, and you will find rest for your souls."

— JEREMIAH 6:16 (NIV)

The dust is still rising. It rises from Galilean shores and Judean deserts. It rises from prison floors and prayer closets. It rises from hospital rooms and refugee camps, from sanctuaries and city streets. It rises wherever a disciple chooses covenant over comfort. It rises wherever a heart whispers, "Yes, I will follow," when the road ahead is unclear. It rises wherever one more set of feet dares to walk behind the Rabbi.

Two thousand years have not stilled the dust. It clung to Simon Peter's sandals when he stumbled after his Rabbi through Gethsemane's shadows. It stained Paul's cloak as he carried the Gospel across Roman roads and prison stones. It laced the prayers of mothers, martyrs, monks, and missionaries — all those who chose the way of surrender. Now it clings to you.

You have not been called merely to admire the footprints. You have been called to make your own.

- Every act of hidden obedience.
- Every prayer whispered when the crowds have scattered.
- Every costly forgiveness, unseen and uncelebrated.
- Every daring, trembling step into unknown places.

They are dustprints. Proof that covenant still burns stronger than comfort. Proof that the Rabbi still leads and that His disciples still follow.

The ancient path is not easy. It never was.

- Some days the road will vanish into wilderness.
- Some days the only light will be the memory of His voice.
- Some days your footprints will mingle with tears, with questions, with aching hope.

But the dust remains. It rises not because the journey is safe — but because it is sacred. It rises because every true disciple, every covenant bearer, walks close enough to the Rabbi to be marked.

This is your heritage now.

- Not the polished gold of worldly success.
- Not the smooth road of cultural applause.

But the ancient road.
The dusty path.
The covenant way.

The Rabbi still leads. The dust still clings. And heaven still leans in to watch whose feet will carry His story into tomorrow's wildernesses, cities, villages, and living rooms.

"Come. Follow Me.
Walk so close that My dust marks your life forever.
Leave a trail others can follow Home."

Walk on, disciple.

Walk through the dust.

Walk into covenant life.

Walk until the day the dust rises no more — because you have followed the Rabbi all the way Home.

ACKNOWLEDGEMENTS

No journey of discipleship is walked alone. This book may bear my name on the cover, but its pages carry the fingerprints and footprints of many who've shaped, sharpened, and strengthened me along the way.

To my wife, Mary—thank you for walking beside me with patience, wisdom, and unshakable love. You are a covenant partner in every sense of the word, and your strength has been a covering through every chapter of our life together.

To my children—Chloe, Nathaniel, Benjamin, and Alyse—your lives remind me daily why this path matters. I pray that your steps will always find the Rabbi's dust and that your hearts will remain soft to His voice.

To my father—thank you for being the first to point me toward the narrow way. Your example of humility, conviction, and unwavering love for Jesus laid the foundation for my own walk. This book exists because you first showed me what it meant to follow.

To my mom, Sally — thank you for being a true family marked not by blood alone, but by grace and steadfastness. I carry your encouragement with me.

To my mentors—Ray Vander Laan, Dr. Eli Lizorkin-Eyzenberg, Dr. Kenneth Bailey, and Max Andrews—your scholarship and spirit have deepened my understanding of Scripture and ignited my love for its Hebraic roots. You helped me see that the Bible is not just a book to be studied, but a story to be lived.

To the students, fellow travelers, and spiritual warriors

who've walked this path with me in study halls, sanctuaries, dojos, and deserts—you've challenged me, prayed with me, and helped shape this message in real life. You are proof that discipleship works when we live it together.

And above all, to the Rabbi Himself—Yeshua, the Messiah.

I am still learning to walk in Your dust. Still stumbling, still surrendering. But I will follow. All the way.

ABOUT THE AUTHOR

Rich Van Doorn is a disciple, teacher, and spiritual pathfinder committed to helping others walk in the dust of the Rabbi. With over four decades of experience in biblical study, martial arts instruction, and faith-based leadership, Rich blends Hebraic scholarship with practical discipleship to awaken a deeper, more covenantal walk with Jesus.

Rich serves as the founder of *The Covenant Path*™—a multi-volume series designed to restore the ancient rhythms of following Yeshua in a world that often forgets the cost. Deeply influenced by the teachings of Ray Vander Laan, Dr. Eli Lizorkin-Eyzenberg, and Dr. Kenneth Bailey, his writing reflects a passion for the Jewish roots of Christianity and the call to live out faith with fierce obedience.

He is also the Grandmaster and Head of School at *Saja Martial Arts*, a Christian martial arts program that trains students to embody courage, humility, and discipline under the banner of Proverbs 28:1: *"The righteous are bold as a lion."*

Rich lives with his wife Mary and their family in the United States, where their home is filled with faith, laughter, and the unshakable belief that every step matters when you walk the path of the Rabbi.

www.ingramcontent.com/pod-product-compliance
Lightning Source LLC
Chambersburg PA
CBHW021323060726
47591CB00006B/1851